The Catholic Parent Wisdom Book

Reminders, suggestions, and majestic thoughts about the most rewarding job in the world

Selected by
Wendy Leifeld

Our Sunday Visitor Publishing Division
Our Sunday Visitor, Inc.
Huntington, Indiana 46750

The publisher is grateful for the use of the materials in this work. If any copyrighted materials have been inadvertently used in this work without proper credit being given in one manner or another, please notify Our Sunday Visitor in writing so that future printings of this work may be corrected accordingly.

Our Sunday Visitor Publishing Division
Our Sunday Visitor, Inc.
200 Noll Plaza
Huntington, Indiana 46750

International Standard Book Number: 96-70437
Library of Congress Catalog Card Number: 0-87973-856-1

Cover design by Monica Watts

PRINTED IN THE UNITED STATES OF AMERICA

856

Contents

Principles for Parents

Before you were conceived
I wanted you.
Before you were born I loved you.
Before you were here an hour
I would die for you.
This is the miracle of life.

—Maureen Hawkins

The most turbulent, the most restless child, has, in the midst of all his faults, something true, ingenuous, and natural, which is of infinite value, and merits every respect.

—Bishop Felix Dupanloup

When you ask too much at first, you often gain nothing at last. And if the heart is lost, all is lost.

—St. Elizabeth Ann Seton

Be first wherever there is a sacrifice to be made, a self-denial to be practiced, or an impetus to be given.

—Amy Carmichael

I call that parent rash and wild
Who'd reason with a six-year-child,
Believing little twigs are bent
By calm considered argument.

—Phyllis McGinley

Who of us is mature enough for offspring before the offspring arrive? The value of marriage is not that adults produce children but that children produce adults.

—Peter De Vries

God sent our children for another purpose than merely to keep up the race — to enlarge our hearts; and to make us unselfish and full of kindly sympathies and affections; to give our souls higher aims; to call out all our faculties to extended enterprise and exertion; and to bring round our firesides bright faces, happy smiles and loving and tender hearts.

—Mary Botham Howitt

Before I got married I had six theories about bringing up children. Now I have six children and no theories.

—John Wilmot (Earl of Rochester)

Children have more need of models than of critics.

—*Joseph Joubert*

It were better for him that a millstone were hanged about his neck, and he cast into the sea, than that he should offend one of these little ones.

—*Luke 17:2*

Do all this little by little, slowly, gently, as the angels do, by pleasing suggestions and without harshness.

—*St. Francis de Sales to St. Jane Frances de Chantal*

Promise little, do much.

—*Hebrew proverb*

It is not any more justifiable to wound the spirit than the body.

—*Shaker saying*

With three things I am delighted, for they are pleasing to the Lord and to men: Harmony among brethren, friendship among neighbors, and the mutual love of husband and wife.

— *Sirach 25:1*

As no child will develop courage by being over protected, so no child will develop it by being pushed.

—*Rollo May*

When a boy is eleven years old you had better find something to engage his interest. I offer it as a theorem that a boy that age is either doing something or breaking something.

—Jerrold R. Zacharias

If there is one mark of perfection, it is simply that it can tolerate the imperfections of others. It is able to adjust. It becomes all things to all men.

—François Fenelon

Let those parents that desire holy children learn to remove silly objects from before them, to magnify nothing but what is great indeed, and to talk of God to them, and of His works and ways before they can either speak or go.

—Thomas Traherne

The wise do as much as they should, not as much as they can.

—French proverb

Remember that the earliest age is the best time to implant that which you wish to have thrive or take deep root in children. And the present time is ever the best time to correct a child for a fault, even while it is fresh in its memory, and can realize the justice of the correction.

—Mother Lucy Wright

Parents learn a lot from their children about coping with life.

—Muriel Spark

At every step the child should be allowed to meet the real experiences of life; the thorns should not be plucked from the roses.

—Ellen Key

The faults of young people,
". . . must be moved by prayer and tears, because they are constitutional and cannot be frightened out."

—St. Elizabeth Ann Seton

There are times when parenthood seems nothing but feeding the hand that bites you.

—Peter De Vries

The joys of parents are secret, and so are their griefs and fears; they cannot utter the one, nor will they utter the other.

—Francis Bacon

We never know the love of the parent until we become parents ourselves.

—*Henry Ward Beecher*

When you are dealing with a child, keep all your wits about you and sit on the floor.

—*Austin O'Malley*

When what you want doesn't happen, learn to want what does.

—*Arabic proverb*

Making a Home

To offer a home to the homeless Christ, start by making your own homes places where peace, happiness and love abound, through your love for each member of your family and for your neighbors.

— Mother Teresa

As the family goes, so goes the nation and so goes the whole world in which we live.

—John Paul II

Of all modern notions, the worst is this: that domesticity is dull. Inside the home, they say, is dead decorum and routine; outside the home is excitement and variety. But the truth is that the home is the only place of liberty, the only spot on earth where a man can alter arrangements suddenly, make an experiment, or indulge in a whim. The home is not the one tame place in a world of adventure; it is the one wild place in a world of rules and set tasks.

—G. K. Chesterton

"She made home happy!" these
few words I read
Within a churchyard, written on
a stone.

—Henry Coyle

There is nothing like staying at home for real comfort.

—Jane Austen

To be a housewife is . . . a difficult, a wrenching, sometimes an ungrateful job if it is looked on only as a job. Regarded as a profession, it is the noblest as it is the most ancient of the catalogue. Let none persuade us differently or the world is lost indeed.

—Phyllis McGinley

Whom God loves, his house is sweet to him.

—Cervantes

Better a dry crust and with it peace than a house full of feasting with strife.

—Proverbs 17:1

Home ought to be our clearing house, the place from which we go forth lessoned and disciplined and ready for life.

—Kathleen Norris

It is the duty of parents to create a family atmosphere inspired by love and devotion to God and their fellow-men. The family is therefore the principal school of the social virtues which are necessary to every society.

—On Christian Education

To be happy at home is the ultimate result of all ambition.

—Samuel Johnson

He is happiest, be he king or peasant, who finds peace in his home.

—Goethe

It was the policy of the good old gentleman to make his children feel that home was the happiest place in the world; and I value this delicious home-feeling as one of the choicest gifts a parent can bestow.

—Washington Irving

Be not a lion at home, nor sly and suspicious at work.

—Sirach 4:30

What is home? A roof to keep out the rain. Four walls to keep out the wind. Floors to keep out the cold. Yes, but home is more than that. It is the laugh of a baby, the song of a mother, the strength of a father. Warmth of living hearts, light from happy eyes, kindness, loyalty, comradeship. Home is first school and first church for young ones, where they learn what is right, what is good and what is kind. Where they go for comfort when they're hurt or sick. Where joy is shared and sorrow eased. Where fathers and mothers are respected and loved. Where children are wanted. Where the simplest food is good enough for kings because it is earned. Where money is not so important as loving-kindness. Where even the teakettle sings from happiness. That is home. God bless it.

—Ernestine Schumann-Heink

A house is no home unless it contains food and fire for the mind as well as for the body.

—Margaret Fuller

Dine on onions, but have a home; reduce your food, but add to your dwelling.

—The Talmud

Let us learn to love in our family. In our own family we may have very poor people and we do not notice them. We have no time to smile, no time to talk to each other. Let us bring that love, that tenderness, into our own home and you will see the difference.

—Mother Teresa

He that flees from his own family has far to travel.

—Petronius

A happy family is but an earlier heaven.

—Sir John Bowring

The family is the place where different generations come together and help one another to grow wiser.

—On the Church in the Modern World

A holy family, that make
Each meal a Supper of the Lord.

—Longfellow

Family bonds are formed less by moments of celebration and of crisis than by the quiet, undramatic accretion of minutiae — the remark on the way out the door. . . the unexpected smile.

—George Howe Colt

The family has the mission to guard, reveal and communicate love, and this is a living reflection of and a real sharing in God's love for humanity and the love of Christ the Lord for the Church His bride. Every particular task of the family is an expression . . . of that fundamental mission.

—*The Role of the Christian Family in the Modern World*

The family is one of nature's masterpieces.

—*George Santayana*

Politeness, that cementer of friendship and soother of enmities, is nowhere so much required, and so frequently outraged, as in family circles.

—*Marguerite Blessington*

I am convinced that more unpleasant feelings are created in families, by these false delicacies, and managements, and hints and go-between friends by courtesy, than ever would have been caused by the parties speaking directly to one another, and telling the plain truth about their thoughts and wishes.

—Maria Edgeworth

Family life is too intimate to be preserved by the spirit of justice. It can be sustained by a spirit of love which goes beyond justice.

—Reinhold Niebuhr

The family you come from isn't as important as the family you're going to have.

—Ring Lardner

God's Children

Concern for the child, even before birth, from the moment of conception and then throughout the years of infancy and youth, is the primary and fundamental test of the relationship of one human being to another.

—*The Role of the Christian Family in the Modern World*

Feel the dignity of a child. Do not feel superior to him, for you are not.

—Robert Henri

We can't form our children on our own concepts; we must take them and love them as God gives them to us.

—Goethe

The soul is healed by being with children.

—Fyodor Dostoevsky

When the first baby laughed for the first time, the laugh broke into a thousand pieces and they all went skipping about, and that was the beginning of fairies.

—James Matthew Barrie

Boyhood is a most complex and incomprehensible thing. Even when one has been through it, one does not understand what it was. A man can never quite understand a boy, even when he has been the boy.

—G.K. Chesterton

You can do anything with children if you only play with them.

—German proverb

Children have never been very good at listening to their elders, but they have never failed to imitate them.

—James Baldwin

Quarrels among boys are harmless, and have more of a pleasant than a bitter character about them. And if boys quickly come to quarrel one with the other, they are easily calmed down again, and quickly come together with even greater friendliness.

—St. Ambrose

With children we must mix gentleness with firmness. They must not always have their own way, but they must not always be thwarted. If we never have headaches through rebuking them, we shall have plenty of heartaches when they grow up.

—Charles Haddon Spurgeon

The discontented child cries for toasted snow.

—Arab proverb

Little girls are the nicest things that happen to people.

—Allan Beck

The child is father of the man.

—William Wordsworth

It is the physical weakness of a baby that makes it seem "innocent," not the quality of its inner life. I myself have seen a baby jealous; it was too young to speak, but it was livid with anger as it watched another baby at the breast.

—St. Augustine

A baby is God's opinion that the world should go on.

—Carl Sandburg

By crawling, a child learns to stand.

—West African proverb

It is dangerous to confuse children with angels.

—David Fyfe

Children in a family are like flowers in a bouquet: there's always one determined to face in an opposite direction from the way the arranger desires.

—Marcelene Cox

There was never a child so lovely that his mother was not glad to get him asleep.

—Ralph Waldo Emerson

Better to be driven out from among men than to be disliked of children.

—Richard Henry Dana

The real menace in dealing with a five-year-old is that in no time at all you begin to sound like a five-year-old.

—Jean Kerr

Children are poor men's riches.

—English proverb

Babies are such a nice way to start people.

—Don Herold

Children have an unerring instinct for knowing when they are being patronized. They go immediately on the defensive against head-patting adults who treat them like strange beings.

—Art Linkletter

Few parents nowadays pay any regard to what their children say to them; the old-fashioned respect for the young is fast dying out.

—Oscar Wilde

Why God Made Mothers

God could not be everywhere and therefore he made mothers.

—Jewish proverb

An ounce of mother is worth a pound of clergy.

—Spanish proverb

A mother is a person who, seeing there are four pieces of pie for five people, promptly announces that she never did care for pie.

—Tennera Jordan

A rich child often sits in a poor mother's lap.

—Danish proverb

If you would reform the world from its errors and vices, begin by enlisting the mothers.

—Charles Simmons

I am changing the world — one diaper at a time.

—Beth Miravalle

Of all the rights of women, the greatest is to be a mother.

—Lin Yutang

The law of labor is more incumbent on a mother than on any other creature; the soul of her child is the field that she ought to cultivate by the "sweat of her brow"; nobody ought to take her place.

—Bishop Felix Dupanloup

The mother's heart is the child's schoolroom.

—Henry Ward Beecher

The mother who spoils her child fattens a serpent.

—Spanish proverb

The mother-child relationship is paradoxical and, in a sense, tragic. It requires the most intense love on the mother's side, yet this very love must help the child grow away from the mother and to become independent.

—*Erich Fromm*

Some wonder that children should be given to young mothers. But what instruction does the babe bring to the mother! She learns patience, self-control, endurance; her very arm grows strong so that she holds the dear burden longer than the father can.

—*Thomas Wentworth Storrow Higginson*

Stories first heard at a mother's knee are never wholly forgotten — a little spring that never quite dries up.

—Giovanni Ruffini

I pray that you will be a warrior and look after children.

—Amy Carmichael

The hand that rocks the cradle rules the world.

—Anonymous

Children are the anchors that hold a mother to life.

—Sophocles

A good mother gives her children
a feeling of trust and stability.
She is the earth. She is the one
they can count on for the things
that matter most of all. She is
their food and their bed and the
extra blanket when it grows cold
in the night; she is their warmth
and their health and their
shelter; she is the one they want
to be near when they cry. . . .
There is no substitute for her.

—Katherine Hathaway

A Father's Touch

Fathers, do not anger your children. Bring them up with the training and instruction befitting the Lord.

—Ephesians 6:4

He that has his father for judge goes safely to trial.

—Cervantes

The most important thing a father can do for his children is to love their mother.

—*Father Theodore Hesburgh, C.S.C.*

One father is worth more than a hundred schoolmasters.

—*George Herbert*

My daddy doesn't work, he just goes to the office; but sometimes he does errands on the way home.

—*Anonymous*

He who has daughters is always a shepherd.

—*Old saying*

When I was a boy of fourteen, my father was so ignorant I could hardly stand to have the old man around. But when I got to be twenty-one, I was astonished at how much he had learned in seven years.

—attributed to Mark Twain

An angry father is most cruel towards himself.

—Publilius Syrus

A platoon leader doesn't get his platoon to go by getting up and shouting and saying, "I am smarter. I am the leader." He gets them to go along with him because they want to do it for him and they believe in him.

—Dwight D. Eisenhower

Happy is the father whose child finds his attempts to amuse it amusing.

—Robert Lynd

To be sure, working — that is earning a living — is one aspect of fathering. It's one means that the father has of extending protection to his family. But it's just one. If he concentrates on this to the exclusion of other aspects, it becomes not a form of fathering, but an escape.

—Myron Brenton

Don't be a lion in your own house.

—Czech proverb

He that loves not his wife or children, feeds a lioness at home and broods a nest of sorrow.

—Jeremy Taylor

In revealing and in reliving on earth the very fatherhood of God, a man is called upon to ensure the harmonious and united development of all the members of the family: he will perform this task by exercising generous responsibility for the life conceived under the heart of the mother, by a more solicitous commitment to education, a task he shares with his wife, by work, which is never a cause of division in the family but promotes its unity and stability, and by the means of the witness he gives of an adult Christian life which effectively introduces the children into the living experience of Christ and the Church.

—*The Role of the Christian Family in the Modern World*

Love's Secrets

Love serves.

—St. Bernard of Clairvaux

The measure of our holiness is not the perfection of our personality or the avoidance of all faults but the extent of our love.

—St. Thomas Aquinas

Untie by love that which your fear has bound.

—*St. Augustine*

All children wear the sign: "I want to be loved — important NOW." Let's read the sign.

—*Dan Pursuitt*

Where there is no love, put in your own and you will draw love out.

—*St. John of the Cross*

The way to love anything is to realize that it might be lost.

—*G.K. Chesterton*

I tell you, that is why her many sins are forgiven — because of her great love. Little is forgiven the one whose love is small.

—*Luke 7:47*

Children need love, especially when they do not deserve it.

—*Harold S. Hulbert*

Married love is an eminently human love because it is an affection between two persons rooted in the will and it embraces the good of the whole person. . . . A love like that, bringing together the human and the divine, leads the partners to a free and mutual giving of self. This love is actually developed and increased by the exercise of it.

—*On the Church in the Modern World*

At the evening of life, you will be examined in love. Learn to love as God desires to be loved and abandon your own ways of acting.

—St. John of the Cross

Love covers a multitude of sins.

—1 Peter 4:8

You know that love cannot be forced on men's hearts, my God, since you created love; it must rather be elicited. And for this further reason that there is no freedom where there is compulsion, and where freedom is lacking — so too, is righteousness.

—William of St. Thierry

In faith and hope the world will
disagree,
But all mankind's concern is
charity.

—*Alexander Pope*

I believe that love is the measure of our ability to bear crosses, whether great or small.

—*St. Teresa of Ávila*

Let all that you do be done in love.

—*1 Corinthians 16:14*

Because of the Lord's great love we are not consumed, for his compassions never fail. They are new every morning, so great is his faithfulness.

—*Lamentations 3:22-23*

Respect is love in plain clothes.

—*Frankie Byrne*

It lies in the nature of conjugal love to be bold, heroic, not to shrink back from taking a risk. All great things on earth are connected with risk. Without risk human life . . . would be deprived of all grandeur and heroism.

—*Dietrich von Hildebrand*

Oh, strong love of God! And how true it is that nothing seems impossible to the one who loves.

—*St. Teresa of Ávila*

Through charity to God we conceive virtues, and through charity toward our neighbors they are brought to the birth.

—*St. Catherine of Siena*

Charity is the reason why anything should be done or left undone, changed or left unchanged; it is the initial principle and the end to which all things should be directed. Whatever is honestly done out of love and in accordance with love, can never be blameworthy. May He then deign to grant us this love, for without it we cannot please Him, and without Him we can do absolutely nothing.

—Blessed Isaac of Stella

For it is love I desire, not sacrifice, and knowledge of God rather than holocausts.

—Hosea 6:6

Teaching the Young

Sow a thought, and you reap an act;
Sow an act, and you reap a habit;
Sow a habit, and you reap a character;
Sow a character, and you reap a destiny.

—*Unknown*

The one who teaches is the giver of eyes.

—*Tamil proverb*

Education — whether its object be children or adults, individuals or an entire people, or even oneself — consists in creating motives. To show what is beneficial, what is obligatory, what is good — that is the task of education.

—*Simone Weil*

You speak of beginning the education of your son. The moment he was able to form an idea his education was already begun.

—*Anna Letitia Barbauld*

The parents exist to teach the child, but they must also learn what the child has to teach them; and the child has a very great deal to teach them.

—Arnold Bennett

All who undertake teaching must be endowed with a deep patience, and, most of all, profound humility. They must perform their work with earnest zeal, that, through their humble prayers, the Lord will find them worthy to become fellow workers with Him in the cause of truth. He will console them in the fulfillment of this most noble duty and finally He will enrich them with the gift of heaven.

—St. Joseph Calasanz

Instruction in youth is like engraving in stone.

—*Moroccan proverb*

To know how to suggest is the great art of teaching.

—*Henri Amiel*

The higher, the more gifted, the more spiritual are minds, the more difficult to shape.

—*Blessed John Henry Newman*

The parents' love is the animating principle inspiring and guiding all concrete educational activity, enriching it with the values of kindness, constancy, goodness, service, disinterestedness, and self-sacrifice.

—*The Role of the Christian Family in the Modern World*

Every boy wants someone older than himself to whom he may go in moods of confidence and yearning. The neglect of this child's want by grown people is a fertile source of suffering.

—Henry Ward Beecher

A good example is the best sermon.

—English proverb

Nothing should be left untried that can train children in early childhood in good morals and in the earnest practice of Christianity. To this end nothing is more effective than pious instructions in Christian doctrine. Children should be entrusted only to good and God-fearing teachers.

—St. John Leonardi

Education does not commence with the alphabet; it begins with a mother's look, with a father's nod of approbation or a sign of reproof; with a sister's gentle pressure of the hand, or a brother's noble act of forbearance; with handfuls of flowers in green dells, on hills, and daisy meadows; with bird's nests admired, but not touched; with creeping ants, and almost imperceptible moments; with humming-bees and glass beehives; with pleasant walks in shady lanes, and with thoughts directed in sweet and kindly tones and words to nature, to beauty, to acts of benevolence, to deeds of virtue, and to the source of all good — to God Himself!

—*Anonymous*

What is learned in the cradle lasts to the grave.

—French proverb

Beware of fatiguing them by ill-judged exactness. If virtue offers itself to the child under a melancholy and constrained aspect, while liberty and license present themselves under an agreeable form, your labor is in vain.

— François Fenelon

I had a good education. I do not mean as to learning; that is only one part of it. I was taught to use my faculties. But, first and best of all, I early learned to seek the favor of God and the approval of conscience.

—Catherine Maria Sedgwick

Education is the knowledge of how to use the whole of oneself. Many men use but one or two faculties out of the score with which they are endowed. A man is educated who knows how to make a tool of every faculty — how to open it, how to keep it sharp, and how to apply it to all practical purposes.

—*Henry Ward Beecher*

It is essential that the student acquire an understanding of and a lively feeling for values. He must acquire a vivid sense of the beautiful and of the morally good. Otherwise he — with his specialized knowledge — more closely resembles a well-trained god than a harmoniously developed person.

—*Albert Einstein*

The roots of education are bitter, but the fruit is sweet.

—*Aristotle*

The education of the child is principally derived from its own observation of the actions, words, voice, and looks of those with whom it lives. The friends of the young, then, cannot be too circumspect in their presence to avoid every and the least appearance of evil.

—*John Jebb*

The "good" child is often more in need of help and attention than the "naughty" child. Because of his aggressiveness the bad boy, so called, is the object of a great deal of concern and counsel while the good lad receives praise or else is overlooked.

—*Karl Menninger*

Parents are . . . through the witness of their lives, the first heralds of the Gospel for their children. Furthermore, by praying with their children, by reading the word of God with them and by introducing them deeply through Christian initiation into the Body of Christ — both the Eucharistic and the ecclesial Body — they become fully parents.

—*The Role of the Christian Family in the Modern World*

Every method of education founded, wholly or in part, on the denial or forgetfulness of original sin and grace, and relying solely on the powers of human nature, is unsound.

—*Pope Pius XI*

Perhaps the most valuable result of all education is the ability to make yourself do the thing you have to do, when it ought to be done, whether you like it or not; it is the first lesson that ought to be learned; and however early a man's training begins, it is probably the last lesson that he learns thoroughly.

—Thomas Henry Huxley

An education which is not religious is atheistic; there is no middle way. If you give to children an account of the world from which God is left out, you are teaching them to understand the world without reference to God. If he is then introduced, he becomes an appendix to his own creation.

—William Temple

Soft Speech, Open Ears

The Law says: "Hear, O Israel, the Lord your God." It does not say: Speak! But, Hear! Eve fell because she said to the man words she had not heard from the Lord her God. The first word God says to you is: Hear!

—St. Ambrose

From the abundance of the heart the mouth speaketh. If your heart is full of love, you will speak of love.

—*Mother Teresa*

A torn jacket is soon mended, but hard words bruise the heart of a child.

—*Henry Wadsworth Longfellow*

Listen, only listen, to my words; this is the consolation you can offer me.

—*Job 21:2*

If a person is without fault in speech he is a man in the fullest sense, because he can control his entire body.

—*James 3:2*

Words should be weighed, not counted.

—*Yiddish proverb*

It was said of Abbot Agatho that for three years he carried a stone in his mouth until he learned to be silent.

—*The Wisdom of the Desert*

I praise loudly, I blame softly.

—*Catherine the Great*

Violence of the tongue is very real — sharper than any knife, wounding and creating bitterness that only the grace of God can heal.

—*Mother Teresa*

Silence is sometimes the answer.

—*Estonian proverb*

Fix your eyes on the Crucified and everything will become small for you. If His Majesty showed us His Love by means of such works and frightful torments, how is it you want to please Him only with words?

—St. Teresa of Ávila

A child tells in the street what its father and mother say at home.

—The Talmud

Speak the truth, but leave immediately after.

—Slovenian proverb

The best remedy I know against sudden fits of impatience is a silence that is gentle and without malice. However little one says, pride always comes into it, and one says things that plunge the heart into grief for a whole day after. When one is silent and smiles in a friendly manner, the storm passes over; one smothers one's temper and indiscretion, and so enjoys pure and lasting happiness.

—St. Francis de Sales

Kind words conquer.

—Tamil proverb

Fathers, do not nag your children, lest they lose heart.

—Colossians 3:21

Let your speech be always with grace, seasoned with salt, that ye may know how ye ought to answer every man.

—*Colossians 4:6*

To scoff at others is one of the worst states a mind can be in. . . . Nothing is so opposed to charity than to despise and condemn one's neighbors. Derision and mockery are always accompanied by scoffing, and it is therefore a very great sin.

—*St. Francis de Sales*

Half the world is composed of people who have something to say and can't, and the other half who have nothing to say and keep on saying it.

—*Robert Frost*

Never reprimand anyone while you feel provoked over a fault that has been committed. Wait until the next day, or even longer. Then make your remonstrance calmly and with a purified intention. You'll gain more with an affectionate word than you ever would from three hours of quarreling. Control your temper.

—*Blessed Josemaría Escrivá*

Speak clearly, if you speak at all; carve every word before you let it fall.

—*Oliver Wendell Holmes*

When you have spoken the word, it reigns over you. When it is unspoken, you reign over it.

—*Arabian proverb*

Family Values

Virtue

Do good and then do it again.

—Welsh proverb

A man never shows his own character so plainly as by the way he portrays another's.

—Jean-Paul Richter

Character is what you are in the dark.

—Dwight L. Moody

Beauty without virtue is a flower without fragrance.

—French saying

The reputation of a thousand years may be determined by the conduct of one hour.

—Japanese proverb

Try not to become a man of success but rather try to become a man of value.

—Albert Einstein

Patience

Patience and time do more than strength or passion.

—*Jean de La Fontaine*

Let us begin by acquiring that patient humility ourselves which we desire so much to see in others, remembering that it is not through the patience and humility of others that we shall be saved, but by our own.

—*Thomas à Kempis*

They also serve who only stand and wait.

—*John Milton*

Patience is power; with time and patience the mulberry leaf becomes silk.

—*Chinese proverb*

Patience with ourselves is a duty for Christians and the only real humility. For it means patience with a growing creature whom God has taken in hand and whose completion he will effect in his own time and way.

—*Evelyn Underhill*

To climb steep hills requires slow pace at first.

—*William Shakespeare*

An elder said: The reason why we do not get anywhere is that we do not know our limits, and we are not patient in carrying out the work we have begun.

—*The Wisdom of the Desert*

Adopt the pace of nature: her secret is patience.

—*Ralph Waldo Emerson*

An aged man, whom Abraham hospitably invited to his tent, refused to join him in prayer to the one God. Learning that he was a fire-worshipper, Abraham drove him from his door. That night, God appeared to Abraham in a vision and said, "I have borne with that ignorant man for seventy years; could you not have patiently suffered him one night?"

—*The Talmud*

Our patience will achieve more than our force.

—*Edmund Burke*

At the gate of patience there is no crowding.

—*Moroccan proverb*

At the bottom of patience one finds heaven.

—*West African proverb*

Self-discipline

The only mortification that was granted me was to master my self-love, and that did me far more good than any bodily penance.

—*St. Thérèse of Lisieux*

Self-respect is the fruit of self-discipline; the sense of dignity grows with the ability to say no to oneself.

—*Abraham Heschel*

Complete abstinence is easier than perfect moderation.

—*St. Augustine*

Perseverance

Strive manfully; habit is overcome by habit.

—Thomas à Kempis

The difference between perseverance and obstinacy is, that one often comes from a strong will, and the other from a strong won't.

—Henry Ward Beecher

Perseverance is more prevailing than violence; and many things which cannot be overcome when they are together yield themselves up when taken little by little.

—Plutarch

Consider the postage stamp, my son. It secures success through its ability to stick to one thing till it gets there.

—*Josh Billings*

By gnawing through a dike, even a rat may drown a nation.

—*Edmund Burke*

Humility

Nothing is difficult for the humble.

—*Blessed Faustina Kowalska*

I long to accomplish a great and noble task, but it is my chief duty to accomplish small tasks as if they were great and noble.

—*Helen Keller*

I'm nobody! Who are you?
Are you nobody, too?
Then there's a pair of us — don't tell!
They'd banish us, you know.

How dreary, to be somebody!
How public, like a frog
To tell your name the livelong day
To an admiring bog!

—Emily Dickinson

The man who said "Blessed is he that expecteth nothing, for he shall not be disappointed," put the eulogy quite inadequately and even falsely. The truth is, "Blessed is he that expecteth nothing, for he shall be gloriously surprised." The man who expects nothing sees redder roses than common men can see, and greener grass and a more startling sun.

—G.K. Chesterton

Generosity

In acts of giving do not fear a lack of means. A generous spirit is itself great wealth. There can be no shortage of material for generosity where it is Christ who feeds and Christ who is fed. In all this activity there is present the hand of him who multiplies the bread by breaking it, and increases it by giving it away.

—*St. Leo the Great*

Many men have been capable of doing a wise thing, more a cunning thing, but very few a generous thing.

—*Alexander Pope*

The fragrance always stays in the hand that gives the rose.

—Hada Bejar

You may light another's candle with your own without loss to yourself.

—Danish proverb

The giver of alms should be free of anxiety and full of joy. His gain will be greatest when he keeps back least for himself.

—St. Leo the Great

The manner of giving is worth more than the gift.

—Pierre Corneille

Delights and Perils of Work

It's not so much how busy you are, but why you are busy. The bee is praised; the mosquito is swatted.

—Marie O'Connor

Alas, I have done nothing this day! What? Have you not lived? It is not only the fundamental but noblest of your occupations.

—*Michel de Montaigne*

My father taught me to work, but not to love it. I never did like to work, and I don't deny it. I'd rather read, tell stories, crack jokes, talk, laugh — anything but work.

—*Abraham Lincoln*

You can work without praying, but it is a bad plan; but you cannot pray in earnest without working.

—*Hudson Taylor*

Nothing is particularly hard if you divide it into small jobs.

—*Henry Ford*

The most obscure and humdrum of human activities are entirely compatible with the perfection of the Son of God. . . . The evangelical holiness proper to a child of God is possible in the ordinary circumstances of a man who is poor and obliged to work for a living.

—René Voillaume

A man who gives his children habits of industry provides for them better than by giving them a fortune.

—Dennis Whately

Mañana is often the busiest day of the week.

—Spanish proverb

Jesus, Saviour, dost thou see
When I'm doing work for Thee?
Common things, not great and
grand,
Carrying stones and earth and
sand?

"I did common work, you know,
Many, many years ago;
And I don't forget. I see
Everything you do for Me."

—children's song by Amy Carmichael

Holiness does not consist in the fervor of love, but in the patience to labor without fervor and to put up with God's delays.

—St. Peter Julian Eymard

Our greatest weariness comes from work not done.

—Eric Hoffer

Amy Carmichael mentioned that she had no doubt cut thousands of small toe- and fingernails — "I who said I would never do any work but 'preach the gospel.' It takes some of us years to learn what preaching the gospel means."

—*quoted by Elisabeth Elliot*

Drones make more noise and work more eagerly than bees, but they make only wax and not honey. So also men who hurry about with tormenting anxiety and eager solicitude never accomplish much, nor do they do it well.

—*St. Francis de Sales*

When one knows how to profit by the least portion of time, one works wonders. . . . This is the art of seizing lost moments — an art which is not learnt from books, but which multiplies and fertilizes time and gives habits of order, attention, and precision which react from the outward to the inward existence!

—*Bishop Felix Dupanloup*

The person who knows God better does God's work more easily.

—*St. Teresa of Ávila*

Nothing is really work unless you would rather be doing something else.

—*James Matthew Barrie*

I like work; it fascinates me. I can sit and look at it for hours.

—Jerome K. Jerome

Man must work. That is certain as the sun. But he may work grudgingly or he may work gratefully; he may work as a man, or he may work as a machine. There is no work so rude, that he may not exalt it; no work so impassive, that he may not breathe a soul into it; no work so dull that he may not enliven it.

—Henry Giles

Labor disgraces no man, but occasionally men disgrace labor.

—Ulysses S. Grant

Work is the greatest thing in the world, so we should always save some of it for tomorrow.

—Don Herold

The harder you work, the harder it is to surrender.

—Vince Lombardi

The world is filled with willing people; some willing to work, the rest willing to let them.

—Robert Frost

For all their works, prayers, and apostolic endeavors, their ordinary married and family life, their daily labor, their mental and physical relaxation, if carried out in the Spirit, and even the hardships of life, if patiently borne — all of these become spiritual sacrifices acceptable to God through Jesus Christ (cf. 1 Pt 2:5). During the celebration of the Eucharist, these sacrifices are most lovingly offered to the Father along with the Lord's body. Thus, as worshippers whose every deed is holy, the laity consecrate the world itself to God.

—*On the Church in the Modern World*

When the Going Gets Tough

This is what God asks of you,
only this:
to act justly, love tenderly, and walk
humbly with your God.

—*Micah 6:8*

Never give in then . . . never admit defeat; keep on working at the Lord's work always, knowing that in the Lord, you cannot be laboring in vain.

—1 Corinthians 15:58

My circumstances are not of my making. One's duty is to act under circumstances. . . . Everything that one does honestly, sincerely, with prayer, with advice, must turn to good.

—Blessed John Henry Newman

God is not unjust, he will not forget your work and the love you have shown him by your service.

—Hebrews 6:10

For the fruit of noble struggles is a glorious one and unfailing is the root of understanding.

—Wisdom 3:15

Depend upon it, the nearer we are to success the more the devil will try to defeat us.

—Blessed John Henry Newman

God will be your immense reward for all eternity, if you persevere faithful to His will.

—Antonio Filicchi to St. Elizabeth Ann Seton

In the divine economy of salvation, no sincere effort remains fruitless even when human eyes can perceive nothing but failures.

—Blessed Edith Stein

An educated man is one who believes he has not succeeded when he has, but is not so sure he has failed when he fails.

—*Lin Yutang*

Courage, my child, let us practice these rough and humiliating, but solid and excellent virtues. Adieu, my child, be quiet, stand on tiptoe, and you will reach to heaven.

—*St. Francis de Sales to St. Jane Frances de Chantal*

A man can fail many times, but he isn't a failure until he begins to blame somebody else.

—*John Burroughs*

Surrender to God, and he will do everything for you.

—*Office of Readings Antiphon, Wk II*

If we take happiness from God's hand, must we not take sorrow, too?

—*Job 2:10*

No one, however weak, is denied a share in the victory of the Cross. No one is beyond the help of the prayer of Christ. His prayer brought benefit to the multitude that raged against Him. How much more does it bring to those who turn to Him in repentance.

—*St. Leo the Great*

Outside God's will there is no true success; in God's will, no failure.

—*Unknown*

God often gives in one brief moment that which he has for a long time denied.

—Thomas à Kempis

All of us are continually faced with a series of great opportunities brilliantly disguised as insoluble problems.

—W.B. Prescott

Because you don't see what can be done, you say God can do nothing — which is like saying there cannot be more within his scope than there is within yours. One thing is clear: if he saw no more than lies within your sight, he could not be God. The very impossibility you see in the thing points to the region God works in.

—George McDonald

Do not make great difficulties out of indifferent matters. Turn your gaze ever so little from yourself and fix it on Jesus Christ.

—*Bishop Jean-Pierre le Camus to St. Louise de Merillac*

We must walk consciously only part way toward our goal, and then leap in the dark to our success.

—*Henry David Thoreau*

"I have done my best." That is all God needs to hear.

—*Unknown*

What's Important and What's Not

Make sure your life does not contradict your words. Sing with your voices, your hearts, your lips and your lives. . . . If you desire to praise Him, then live what you express. Live good lives and you yourselves will be his praise.

—St. Augustine

Faithfulness, not success.

—Mother Teresa

Nothing recedes like success.

—Winston Churchill

He will be the sure foundation for your times, a rich store of salvation and wisdom and knowledge; the fear of the Lord is the key to this treasure.

—Isaiah 33:6

People need joy quite as much as clothing.

—Margaret Collier Graham

The figure of the Crucified invalidates all thought which takes success for its standard.

—Dietrich Bonhoeffer

Even on the most exalted throne in the world we are only sitting on our own bottom.

—Michel de Montaigne

The logic of worldly success rests on a fallacy: the strange error that our perfection depends on the thoughts and opinions and applause of other men! A weird life it is, indeed, to be living always in somebody else's imagination, as if that were the only place in which one could at last become real!

—Thomas Merton

I don't know the key to success, but the key to failure is trying to please everybody.

—Bill Cosby

What does it profit you to give God one thing if He asks of you another? Consider what it is that God wants and then do it. You will, as a result, better satisfy your heart than with that toward which you yourself are inclined.

—*St. John of the Cross*

There are only two lasting bequests we can hope to give to our children. One is roots, the other, wings.

—*Hodding Carter*

You cannot buy an inch of time with an inch of gold.

—*Chinese proverb*

What have you to fear from a hand that was pierced and nailed to the cross for you?

—Blessed Claude de la Colombière, S.J.

All the treasures of the earth cannot bring back one lost moment.

—French proverb

There is no hand to catch time.

—Bengali proverb

Those mercies are the sweetest that we enjoy after waiting and praying for them.

—Elizabeth Dunton

The serene silent beauty of a holy life is the most powerful influence in the world, next to the might of the Spirit of God.

—Blaise Pascal

One ought, every day at least, to hear a little song, read a good poem, see a fine picture, and, if it is well possible, to speak a few reasonable words.

—Goethe

For anything worth having one must pay the price; and the price is always work, patience, love, self-sacrifice — no paper currency, no promises to pay, but the gold of real service.

—John Burroughs

Accusing the times is but excusing ourselves.

—English proverb

The secret of success is constancy of purpose.

—Benjamin Disraeli

It doesn't matter, really, how great the pressure is, it only matters where the pressure lies. See that it never comes between you and the Lord — then, the greater the pressure, the more it presses you to His breast.

—Hudson Taylor